Poets' Choice®



deMichelle

# Coventry, Recovery and Me: The Anger I Hide

Edited by Daniel Rosario

Published By

Poets' Choice®

Poets Choice and Free Spirit LLC
*1216 Broadway Floor 2 PMB 1010 - New York NY 10001 - USA*

www.poetschoice.in
Phone: +1 914-650-2747 (Primary) + 1 646 974 9406 (Fax)

1st Edition Oct 2025

Edited by Daniel Rosario

Printed in India

ISBN: 978-93-6617-270-5
BCID: 983-17674706

Visit www.bookcrossing.com

Instagram - *@freespiritpublisher*
Youtube - *@freespiritpublisher*

Contents

***One day you will tell your story***

*of how you overcame what you went through,*
*and it will be someone else's survival guide*

*Brene Brown*

# *No one is more hated than he who speaks the truth*

*Plato*

When writing about what I am going through,
while I am going through it, I am writing about myself
Because that is a promise I make to all the readers
with whom I intend to share my words.
The word *You* could be defined as
all the members of my extended families
over the last 50 years of my life.
Those people, within circles, who
would qualify into categories
of which I cannot speak.
*You* is intended for my readers who
find themselves feeling as if
they have always been brutally trampled
and can find no other way out.
*You* could suggest those people who
exercise their covert manipulation

and well-mastered control upon *us*

because we serve

as fodder for their souls.

*You* is applied to anybody

who is not otherwise identified.

Therefore, my words

can now be appreciated as

*ME* addressing *YOU.*

Anybody who does not qualify with *me*,

should read and decide for themselves

if they are or are not part of the categories

of which I cannot speak.

# COVENTRY

# *My Muse, My Lake*

This writing is amazing to me; I do not even think
The words enter my mind and flow fluidly through my hand
Who would have thought pen and ink would be the path I would have chosen?
But here it is and here I go: so much to say
My high sensitivity is getting in my way
When typing the words I write, I get a migraine
The wealthy sunlight wears me down, the backlight does me in.
Arthritis makes this hard to read, yet the thoughts just come again
Perhaps these thoughts that burden me have been here all along
Perhaps they are still silenced and coming through just now.
Either way, I will write until my mind slows down.

Fifty years of misery are surfacing here and now.
In this moment I feel nothing to identify.
Perhaps each feeling presents itself, pushing me to write.
To think, to decipher, to process as I never have before.
The hole in me is closing up; that I can feel.
Wouldn't it be wonderful if I were to find an end.
An end to my own dissention, encouragement found.
This process moves in that way, I know it does, and I'm ready for a break.
It is beautiful outside; the lake, it calls me in,
I will go sit down with it and thank it once again.
Dismissed, diminished, delusional are the words I must move past.
I'm getting there, I know I will, to love, peace, and success.

# *In The Moment*

5:15 a.m. on a July Friday morning

Waking slowly, rumination, avoiding

Hypnosis of overnight bruxism

Relaxation slowly found me

The cabin is coming back to life

Today peaceful, quiet, undisturbed

Visit to the lake

What will this morning bring?

Clouds for now

Library trip planned

Organize and tidy these rooms

which finally feel like home

Looking forward to

A weekend at the ranch

Fridays are now freeing

No rush, no hurry up and write

Meditation music soothes my soul

Much typing for the weekend

Much love and peace lie in store

Fridays are no longer the release they used to be

Just a warm and comforting time

This week has been productive

Let's see what this Friday brings

# RECOVERY

## *from I JUST AM*

# *I Just Was*

Traumas, expanding like the wake,

So much stronger than the lake,

Working toward the shore

I am here, yet, I am not, I am a distant afterthought,

I sit, I observe, I wonder not, I am drama wrought

I was here, I wrote these words

I cannot thrive, I am distraught

I've never asked for very much,

I see the kids surrounding me,

I study looks upon their faces,

I wonder what, inside of them,

causes each look to change, it is strange.

I am absent, my statement is made, which gives way

to the inward assumption that...

*...I Just Was*

# *Neglect*

Neglect cannot be written.

It's in a place unknown.

It's the absence of a presence.

A suppressed need unknown.

As for me when nothing was.

That which was, was not.

A word of inattention,

to an absent want.

Desideratum unrequited,

obligations left to choice.

A person's drought unsatisfied

One who has no voice.

A mind who speaks about all things

thought, to thought, to thought,

Were I to say remember,

one might say u huh.

But to those words beyond what's said
one hears a meaning not.
Motive and intention,
below the rug is swept.

When one gives in to wonder,
souls' matter is in reach.
Meanings now to every word.
To every song you hear.

Was this one not encouraged,
to speak what's in his heart?
One could not give meaning to
a poem laced with art.

The words are not cohesive,
the sentiment is tossed.
I think the words, I say the words,
these words, too, have meaning not.

Thinking of a person
whom another's lost,
does not bring feeling to the soul
about those who must go on.

Blessed by keeping all things out,
which leaves none left inside.
Innocence and wonderment want foundation
upon which thoughts can reside.

How does one give feeling,
to the word of love,
when love is not a feeling
in neither heart nor soul?

One cannot profess to love,
when love's an abstract word.
I hear of love, I say I love, yet I need none in return.
One never knew one's own self-love.

He does not see inside himself,
where intimate passion lies?
The absence of recession.
Has he ever felt his soul?

I've loved this man so very much.
I believed he loved me, too.
He can't give meaning to the word,
so, no love follows through.

Without expectation,
wants, thoughts or needs.
When love is not the soul of one,
one feels its soul recede.

One may miss the times and habits.
Never the absence of....
One cannot bear witness to
words never told in full.

I question not the words in use,
I question their intent.
Does a person raised as such
embrace this element?

Seeing her with someone new,
a devastating loss.
The pain was unpredicted,
his heart and soul were wrought.

Moving on meant much to him,
it was the next best step.
But the feeling of diminishment
left him with loss to accept.

So, for him, I speak a poem,
of love's strength and its loss.
The loss of what the future held.
About the course of us.

Be strong, please, my man, I know

the champion that you are.

Be brave beyond what you've just felt,

And embrace it, **soul** and **heart**.

# *Forevermore*

Where is my voice, where does it lie,

I know the topic, which begs me to say,

It's urgent, it's current, it wants the world to know

Who I am inside

Who I am inside is silenced.

Yet, I live on

The future that I'm reaching for,

just beyond my grasp

Dangling there in front of me calling me by name

I reach for it, it says come here

The past that always follows me

Wraps its arm tightly and tells me, don't you dare

A pressure in my shoulders telling me to fight

Push forward, push forward

The book sits here upon the floor trading my fears with hope

My book, this book, my heart and my soul

Begging me to just hold on,

speaks on its own behalf

Were I to be read, my tears would soak the binding

My heart, I believe, would rejoice

That somebody out there hears me

Somebody hears my voice

Or, if they don't yet, they will

I am begging here inside myself

To find someone who shares my strife

Unlikely though, my story's odd, but wouldn't it feel wonderful

To find someone who believes I stand a chance

To tell the world it sucks in here, inside these book-bound walls

I am here, yes, I am, I'm here, let me be free,

Release this writing from the pen

Perhaps the words would then

Make way for pleasanter notes

Waiting  to be penned

Lightness, weightlessness

I know it's there, it's in those fingertips

I'm reaching....

Reaching...

Reaching for, reaching strong, never letting up.

This story here which none could share, please believe me, there really is

She, the one who pens these words, has laid it on the line

She wrote me, this book, you see,

The wait has been too much

Too much for this urgent dialogue to sit and rest, not nearly at peace.

The only thing stronger than fear...

...fear of the ultimate dismissal,

...fear that as, within her world, nobody cares

The only thing stronger than fear is hope

I'll hope, I'll hope, I'll hope

This book, this me, the words I scream

Have no other choice, just hope

Queries out, a multitude

Poems, essays, into comps

No word, no word, no word

I wish that I could stomp upon the folks who've passed me by

Once again, I'll scream, I'll keep screaming on the pen's behalf

Until I finally feel heard

The pen and she who holds it have never felt heard

My pen, this pen, has been heard but,

until my words are shared,

That's just not enough

Narcissism, sociopathy, twelve traumas to survive

Who in the world would fit that bill?

Just me, this book, lying on the floor

I'd like to put my story forward and witness that release,

Inside the person's body, oh, how she will weep

She'll cry the tears that have been trapped in me and inside her

In these written words.

She'll cry 'til night is day,

She'll cry so long we won't believe
Releasing pent-up demons
Which, until now, have lain deep, down, beneath
fifty years of conflict in which written words were honed
Dismissed, diminished, beaten down
This is what she writes
She wrote my words, pain to release
yet the pain goes on,
It sits inside this pen's soul
Trying desperately,
Waiting, not so patiently,
For the written words to trap, embrace, discern, disgust,
dismiss, and to destroy
To be diminished as has always been her soul,
and then to release and rest
Granted the peace that has been a lifetime earned
Perhaps a poetry book would bring her from there to
here
The method she knows best
She's written this so fluidly I am surprised

Pen and paper from way back when,
seems to be her newfound source
To share her words
with others now
Perhaps this book takes one step back
And gets out of the way
She clearly has so much to say
let this begin the way
The topic that she knows the best
To be the start of something prosperous to make her words be heard
This poem goes on endlessly
Theres always more to say
Help her find her voice again
The one she had way back when
Before the man of hushed denial
threw all her words away
Her heart, her soul, her identity
Many years of urgency
precede these words, you know

To the pen it's time for me to say "hello"

I love my book so honestly but cannot wait much more

I must say what I must say, readily

Here's to my first option

My poetry to bridge the gap between.

My mind, it slows now, it's content

That one way or another

these words will soon get out

They are out of me,

They will sit right here for now

share them with the world I must

This has gone on too long

I will write and write until

The written word is heard

# *Where My Feelings Hide*

My feelings have been forced back in
I have feelings without names
Dismissed or diminished, it matters not
        I still have them
Any words about feelings I have ever heard are spoken with derision
        Yet, I still feel them
I am a poem, an unspoken, intended emotion
Emotion that serves me best in written word
Shut me down and I will freeze,
But when a little butterfly evokes the warmth within
When the strength of the caterpillar creates new days of beauty
And my heart feels their heart, that heart, its heart
Both speechless, it and I, but connected through the feelings that remain within

The uplifting of the butterfly's soul as it spreads its wings to glide

It allows itself to be carried with the breeze through worlds yet unexplored

The world yet unexplored,

It touches my soul,

The self-imposed sense of letting go of what has always been

To truly appreciate what has yet to come

The inert understanding of our connection, this butterfly and I,

And a link to all the things that are alive in nature and remind me of

## Where my Feelings Hide

Deep, down

Where my feelings hide

Where do they hide? I will never know.

Where is that...my deep down

Where is it in my body

When I reach for it, from where will an emotion come,

when a song mentions a sunrise,

Where does my body reach to bless me with the feeling

that a sunrise should allow?

I can feel it in my heart

Where does it search when the vision of the moon at

night pulls me forward and allows

me to feel what the darkening of the sky is intended to

make me feel?

I can feel it in my soul

Where does it reach when poetry draws me into

something

That I can feel but cannot yet define

What will change when these feelings are finally defined?

Nothing. Because I always feel them.

A feeling is a feeling, dismiss it if you will,

But I will still be feeling it long after you deride

I still have these feelings that cannot be diminished

Words are dismissed, words are diminished

A feeling is a feeling and that can never be changed

Try as you may

# *Disposition*

My room, my cottage, my solitary life
Takes me back to the days long past
When I hid inside my room
The attic up above
And wrote down everything I felt
I let my heart release
Into written words on paper
Pen in hand
Onto paper clean
All the feelings that I'd felt
        Ever in my life
Found their way, somehow,
to be penned and come alive
I wrote and saved my poetry
In a notebook, properly categorized
When, now married, I went for them
They were no longer there

To the man with whom I lived,

There just he and I,

He, knowing where they'd been kept,

Confronted by me

'You don't need them', is what he said

What did you do with them,

Give them back to me please.

You didn't throw them away, did you.

A shrug of hushed denial

I collapsed, felt defeated.

My everything was gone

If I thought you had a soul

Remorse, or even empathy

I'd ask you to think back again

To feel what my heart felt that day

When you disposed of my heartbeat

Me reaching toward my whole and

Who I'd always been.

Take it, stomp it, crush it beyond belief

Like your mother had done to you

The baseball cards, yes

Why I didn't leave you then

I truly cannot say

Instead I thought, what's done is done,

There was no recourse

There was no responsibility to enforce

Because who else would have known

That I had poetry, written and saved

So, it would be that only he

Knew what he

Had gone and done.

So, instead I pushed it way, way down

Below the depths of my soul

Below every feeling wrongly felt

Below my traumas,

Below whatever would come next

And left it there to eat at me...

Forevermore.

# Listening

I know, now, what to say about my life gone bad
It's short, unsweet, and to the point
Listening in my world never has been done
It's a bridge that's insurmountable, men don't see the need
To stop the chatter in their minds and listen.
More can be said, no doubt, I'm sure,
But my words will never be heard and neither then, will I
My dad's a different person, not bred from some ill will
He will listen, he will hear me.
But once he does, what should I expect
Early eighties, dismissed, diminished, beaten down
Just like me.
We are both the same.
And this word, same, feels comforting
No ill will to be shared
Once reminded that as a habit,

he is defending rotten seeds.

He will stop what he is doing and listen with intent.

I expect nothing from him but to understand

It is not him that I avoid,

It's the women's thumbs that we've been enslaven to

That necessitate this no-contact policy

That I implement

There is no hatred, no ill will, just distance to save my soul,

My heart, my mind, my life. To save my sanity.

He I think would understand the words that I just said

Unless these women get to him first and desecrate my name

That is where our problem lies.

The ladies must be in command and speak louder than I have

Until my voice has been drowned out

So they can tell my father

what he should think, should need, should want, should feel

Convincing him that he is too old to understand
Sparing him the lot of that is my saving grace,
My sister has plowed through everything that intel can provide.
Should they need me, Mom and Dad
I'll be there in no time
They have my email, we stay in touch, I'm not hard to find.

# *Hearing*

That poem, there, on the last page
Holds the solution to my riddle.
Should one not know just what I need
It's right there. Learn to listen.
When one listens and responds appropriately
I should then feel heard.
Not just one and done, though, consistently
So much so that I can expect
To be heard every time I try
No dismissal, no diminishment, sit quietly and take it in
Here is where one's problem lies, turn off the chatter in your head
That, at my third word, is already constructing your response.
The best response would always be, Yes, I understand.
But do you, though, understand,
Or will you now walk away?

As if that exchange had never happened, at all

Learn to understand,

Learn to relate to others

Me, of course, and then everyone,

Your problems could be solved

Were you to not understand this point that I have made

Would validate, for me, what's already in my mind,

No empathy.

# *She Laughs*

Strong words, confused and abused
Dismissed and buried in a hurry, absent life, empty me
Tears, many tears, flip that switch, to an extreme, wailing, balling,
Nowhere to turn, no light to burn
Something is missing, but what?
Feeling stupid, that laugh, intense and punishing,
I know...she laughs, no recognition,
I think...she laughs, no discourse,
I see...she laughs, no empathy
I'm sad...she laughs, no remorse
I am sad...she laughs, laughs, laughs
I'm scared, confused, dismissed, diminished
I ache...odd silence, will she walk away?
    Come with me, come with me, she says
    Nevermind that, come with me,
    You belong here! You stay near! I adhere...upon

command

Still confused and abused, used but then, again, for

what?

I know, I think, I see, I hurt, I'm sad,

Laugh, laugh, laugh

Laughter that has now gone mad

Love of self, never taught, pushed aside and drama

wrought

No sense of me

Something is wrong, I know not

What makes me whole, I know not

I will survive, I know not how

I stub my toe...everlasting roars of laughter

I trip and laugh galore

Laugh, laugh, laugh

Floating, circling, crushing

Quiet that laugh and hear me both now and...

...forevermore

# The Claw

When B, you have a point to make don't approach me with your claw.

That you will pound into my chest to prove you know it all.

The pounding will not end until I fake agree

that you must certainly be right.

The pounding stops immediately.

Done. Just like that.

If you pound into my chest until you get the answer that you need

Are you really in control or, by faking, are we?

Pound away and I will fake every single time.

I know I will, I'm in control of me. Always, now.

I've seen you say in text:

"I am my own worst enemy."

The thing is I am not; no contact is my only viable strategy.

The best one I can find, to keep peace in my mind,

And leave your pretend control behind.

"I left my home, my family, it's no wonder I'm alone.

Until (my) one friend catches on to (me)

And then she'll be gone."

That's just it, again. She is here.

You are not. Peace has been maintained.

I give her no reason to want to run

but you do

Every chance you can.

"You're a good author. You don't need to write a book to prove it."

Don't I though, isn't that what authors do?

Nice try, I see

Perhaps, then, I couldn't say anything about you, I see.

A no contact policy in place but the dissertations linger

And get longer each time.

This time there's no pounding.

Just smiling because I know you're afraid,

And you've retreated

to your 'cave'.

To hide

The pounding took place throughout my life

I HAVE HAD ENOUGH!

You don't know all, no one does, but through your voice,

you think you do

Would I try to divert you, you'd follow my every turn

Pound, pound, pound...enough, enough

Omnipotence cannot be held by anyone here on earth.

When I say "you must be right" you don't laugh at me.

Why is that sentence the only thing you hear?

You fall silent, you sit, conversation over.

But then I look at you and

Laugh, laugh, laugh.

No words, just laugh.

When you poke, and when you laugh

Know that is why we're done,

now, and...

... forevermore.

# Coversion

We have distance, we live apart, cousin B and me,

I am here at water's edge as happy as can be.

The rumor mill from my hometown says

I must be delusional.

I think we will, both, my reader and me,

Get a laugh at that, for we have learned.

There are people who throw tantrums

when they fear that they will be drawn out

As the square peg trying to fit into the round hole.

Communication between me and cousin B

Which is limited for reason, is a rare text message,

Temporarily unblocked

Dissertation from the other source to me

About all my flaws, on and on and on

Aw, thank you, hun, that's exactly what I need.

Direction and demands…NOT

Who do we know that behaves like you

I believe it's Anty J

You'll want to tell Cousin K. She'll email me tomorrow.

When text is done, I block, again, and save the contents

For when she pushes me too far

We all know it will come

When and where I will not know she has a talent for popping up

Out of place, out of time, in my face...here I am.

Face to face will be the place where she sets the words upon

My wounded, broken, tattered, soul and pushes me to defend

I won't defend anymore; there never was any point.

Dissertate, dissertate, uh huh, uh huh, uh huh

When I find a creative way to sneak away unscathed

I will close my door and say, that's it, she's done, again

Life experience dictates, she'll have a smile on her face

In her mind she's defeated me

In mine, fake, fake, fake and...

...a laugh all my own

Diminishment can go away

Freedom, now, is still all mine,

there's nothing she can say

She has no sword, she's helpless now,

I believe she's always been.

I am not beneath her thumb anymore.

Peace for sanity's sake.

What she did not understand

While she manipulated my mind

My pen has always been mightier than...

...her words

...her weaknesses

...what's telescoped onto me

Not anymore.

I, your self-entitled source of self-esteem...

...has gladly walked away.

# Loss

After my second pregnancy, of which there were three,
Two healthy births and, between them both, I miscarried
Being the person who gives all of me to satisfy all needs
of others,
I can't help but wonder why no one cares for me?
Why, when I miscarried, did my world go silent?
Thanksgiving dinner, hormones still at play
Vision of that moment still haunting me today,
I cried all day.
Why did no one say a word to me?
Even the attention hog was silent.
And I have never felt so alone.
No laughs, no pokes,
Heartbroken and alone
Having lost my baby was an interruption to the life that
I'd already planned.

I wouldn't hold my baby, names still rolling through my mind.

Loss of anticipation crushed me.

Loss of life those plans were for.

One child running around now, thank goodness, that

I felt the loss of every moment

That I'd just shared with boy

And should have had again

Nobody spoke. Not even a word.

If you can't say something nice, don't say anything at all.

Would that mean that there was nothing nice to say?

I don't believe that's true.

Were the roles reversed I would easily have found

Many nice words to use.

I'm sorry for your loss, if nothing else

Blanketed words saved for last rites.

Would be perceived as nice

In the eyes of a person, for whom the loss can still be felt.

Leaving there that day and making my way home

I was confronted with new words when the door was closed.

‘What the eff is wrong with you? We will effin try again?”

More barked than effin said.

I went back to my bedroom, alone, again

To be away from him.

Being alone with me

Was the only safe place to be

# *What About Me*

Have I ever phrased my words with a tone that would
imply
Or even sound like it should be one
 that should end with the words
  What about me?
Life experience has taught me to recognize
words which end and leave room for the words
What about me?
 Even though those words are never spoken aloud.
Anty L, I have an illness, any malady at all,
Next words will speak the same.
Say, pain in my stomach, because
On this day, I really do, but
The response comes back oh no. oh my.
Have you called the doctor
I say yes and it is over
This time yet once again

Relaxing into talking, nothing pertinent to say,

None to be considered

She called the doctor...OK

On another occasion,

Were I to make mention to no one in particular

“How do I not know?” Anty L says

“Why don’t you tell me these things.”

“I believe I should know”

Unspoken words, the “what about me?”

One year at dance, a demonstration

My daughter danced, as well.

Our family came.

After the show,

in the studio where I worked

Back at my desk wishing everyone farewell.

“That was nice. I should have done it when I had the chance.”

“It’s rewarding,” I’d said.

“I should have done it when I had the chance.”

Good way to turn everyone’s hard work

into something about you,

What about you?

At Christmas she sat down next to me with papers in her hand

She wanted me to ask about them, so I didn't dare

She mentioned my strokes and said

"It's different when you're our age and expecting it."

"I guess," said I.

"It's different when you're our age..."

Mmm, hmm

Of course, because, what about you?

Theres nothing to contend with, it's harmless if I choose it.

Newborn me, couldn't reason that out

Youth, preteen, the teens with no understanding

Leaves doubt and sincere concern for

The intended "what about me?"

"Worry!" she says

"I am entitled. I'll worry when I will.

I want to worry," far more barked than said

I get it, what about you?

There are a million things in life we cannot control

Worry paves no path, except now the world can know.

She is worried. Not of the illness.

Of the torture it places on her.

What wrath this illness has been put upon,

Simply, because, what about me?

When she was lying awake last night, the ill were sound asleep

She shared her worry with everyone, and yet, the ill received no weep

# *How Can You See?*

High in sensitivity, light and I don't get along
My blinds are all closed, study light behind my head,
Were Anty L to see me now, she'd ask, "How do you see?"
Turn on two more lights and open the blinds in full
Now, I'm blinded. Now I'm done.
My headache for thirty years might just be explained.
Blinding sunlight does not help me see,
It gives me reason to keep my eyes closed…
For eighty years, how do you see?
Has haunted me, distracted me,
Blinded me.
Barking commands moves the attention in the room
To her, of course.
Upstairs, my bedroom, window one,
No surprise I'd hide in there
With my guilt and shame and fear
Broad daylight weighs me down

Backlight does me in

Dark and cool is how I like it.

Dark and cool is how it is.

# *Blind Obedience*

If now, I had the two of you here today with me
Anty L and cousin B
This hand would tire to push past the pain.
Oh, what would I say to you that has not been said
before?
Nothing. Nothing.
What then would I say to you that's never been heard
before?
Anything. Everything.
You take pride in the vision that paints you both the
same
Which, to you, means you're okay
Perfect in every way
Omnipotence is not possible, but I know you'll disagree.
The minion and the mouse in me beg you take your
leave.
You both have strangled who I am inside

And who I could have been.

For want of blind obedience

And silence of my soul

Words I spoke diminished,

Physical pain, as well, dismissed

There was nothing there important

Obsolescence.

A need for attention must be the cause.

Had it occurred to either of you, at all

Perhaps my need to be attended to

Was because it had never crossed your mind

If a need for attention is nature-born

Then surely, so is the magic to bring it forth.

Your imposed intent to dismiss me of attention

Was the last punch in a series of grapples

Over my lack of attention and then, of that, my need

Which was nobody's fault, you'd say

Untrue.

Perhaps the rolling eyes, the crossing of arms, the pivot
and the walkaway

Rather than teaching me to shut myself up

Taught me, that I was right.

You didn't then, you wouldn't now, and I'm way out of line.

Sad and hurtful.

Perhaps the verbal dissertations

While, controlling, mean and vain

Left me with an absence of attention

That I should have already been paid.

Not a newfound gimmick, pain.

Each gathering, one week before, my body would respond

To the absence, dismissal and ignorance

I knew that I'd be dealt.

You made me sick, every single time.

Dissertations meant to shut me up

And leave me with no recourse

Cut deep in mind, to be held forevermore.

I knew from that what to expect

And I sought a different course.

Perhaps that mirror image

While, to you equates perfection

Means you both demand,

power overall.

Thus, impugning my neglect

Once dismissed, diminished, broken down

Once adhered with no dissent

I had shut my mouth, I waited

Turned and walked away.

Away from the witches brew boiling in the cave

Surrounded by the monkeys

Who blindly will obey

your every wish

When sent out to wreak havoc

While you retreat into the land

Caressing the ball, erasing it all,

Behold the wrath is at your command.

Telling the ball to vanquish me

Before I've time to share

Before I tell the world around

You are not who you seem

You know not, you think not

Caress the ball and wait

You are not to be believed

My diminishment must play its course

Before I'm made aware

My ruby slippers have a magic

Unaware

They will take me to reality with

Five little spoken words

And they'd be right, because

There truly is no place like *my* home

Take me away from the fiction at hand

It was just a dream.

Voiced from within the absence that

You both took much time to create

My heart and soul imagined you

I then must be delusional

Something must be wrong with me

That it is your power that I wish to relieve.

If I speak up, this pail I hold

Will be used to your remiss

You will both together

melt and disappear

The monkeys, they will turn on you

Not so blind, after all

Because their thoughts have been averred

To believe that I was broken

Had always been so wrong.

They were just afraid of you.

You'd achieved the blind obedience and silence of my soul.

Admission now that omnipotence was never yours at all

You dismissed respect to inflict fear

Of everything around

The quiet, silenced, mouse in me knew that all along

But knew better than to address your flaws,

go no contact,

And disappear.

I am not delusional

I was up against a thick, stoned wall
That hid the wicked within.
The two who reigned above us all
Have melted in the wash.
They hold us not, anymore
Truth is…they never did.

Writing about my feelings has become
Nonsense to them both.
One other is protected, from my chaos,
This all makes no sense to one
Who has no place within
To think about another's heart
Or the waves that wane within
Thank you, ladies, for that validation
It all speaks my thoughts so clear
It tells me that I am on track
And following the proper path
My words cause chaos to persons
Who cannot reach into themselves

To find their own emotions,

empathy or remorse

I've often wondered if you two had both of those,

Today, I know, without a doubt

To label me delusional will only work for a short time.

Because, sooner or later, I will appear

And my soul will show clearly through

One cannot be delusional, purely on a certain whim.

When I make full sense to others,

Your walls will crash again.

Melted as you are, yet stubborn as can be,

You will no longer silence me

While I write out what I feel.

This writing is a path that you had not foreseen

And I will embrace it just as much

As I always have

My nonsense feelings and chaotic words

Will appear where they should, when they should

Because I hope you see my friends,

my pen has always been...

...mightier than your words.

# from TRAUMA

# *Rage*

I was born with sin in my mouth, sin, undefined,
Not the silver spoon with which
Cousin B was blessed,
I am stigmatized
Cousin B says my written words are nonsense
She tells cousin K, my spoken words cause chaos,
She says I'm delusional and some monkeys hop aboard.
My feelings used to be hard to reach
Let alone put into words
Back in the day,
Yet here I am.
I cannot be silenced, anymore

I've lived a paranormal existence
Like a shadow in the corner
Eyeing the world around me
Hiding like a ghost

Silent as a mouse until

The rising sun

I was subverted by the moonlight

Different in the light of day

I was an unwanted obligation

Which threw my mother's love

To the child who went before

The one who is just like her

What if "just like her" is not the best thing to be?

Disorder begets disorder, control begets control,

Dismissal, diminishment, derision,

Squashing, crushing, silencing,

Then comes another firm footprint,

Defined by the mother's beloved.

You'd think I'd wish to be like her

But I don't

Disorder begets disorder, control begets control

My scapegoat is a side effect of both.

In control,

They can't be held responsible for much

So they assign another to bear the weight

of their errors and misdeeds

I am not responsible for others' misdeeds and errors

Though they believe I am.

Disorder begets disorder, control begets control

I am not your pincushion

No, not anymore

Your behaviors are your own

Your errors are yours, as well

Now that the scapegoat removes herself

She is held onto through the children she loves

To bear the weight of disorders, to suffer the control

No, not anymore

Disorder begets disorder, control begets control,

My kids, cousin B, isn't after you

She is after me and using you to reach me.

She's using you to break my heart

At least, that's what she believes

To discredit everything I say.

She shares with you her silver spoon

When each time she pulls it out,

She is using it to beat you down.

I used to say your relationship with her

Was different than my own,

And agreed it was okay.

That is not true, anymore.

You believe the commands she is making

Beat, beat, beat...because she cares

Disorder begets disorder, control begets control,

Control is used to beat you down

Beat, Beat Beat...because she cares

What she thinks you should believe

The words she chooses are not hidden.

When and how she uses them is covertly structured.

Beat, Beat, Beat...because she cares

They are right there in front of you.

I'm sorry she has chosen you.

To say what she won't dare say

For fear of being found out publicly

Disorder begets disorder, control begets control

Believe that I am right next to you

The wrath, it must ensue.

I'm sorry that you've been pulled in

That was not my goal.

I've put distance between me and her

To find peace for sanity's sake

Love begets love

I know you've been lured away

When the flaw in her logic stands out for you to see

Family begets family

Reach out to me.

# *Magnet*

Neglect, abuse, molestation, rape, and ASPD perhaps

The story of my life is the story of a mind, soul and heart.

I never speak my feelings out

Conditioned as I have been

If I do, I first accept that they will not be heard

Nor responded to appropriately

If at all

I read those first six words

And think about who I could have been

Which hadn't occurred to me at all, back then

I am the mouse inside the wall

Fetching cheese right quick

Then hiding back inside the wall

Chewing while I can

That mouse should have a story

Of who she used to be

But my story twists and turns

In and among itself

What is it then that I've become

A poet and author proud,

Of surviving all the traumas

Not knowing

Eight more were yet to come

Trauma twelve—a bout with cancer

Early prediction did its job

My one year apart mammograms

Stage 1A and surgery

The surgery repeated three times

To find a clear margin.

I chose to focus on

How well she was paying attention

Cancer-free at eighteen months

Into five years of medication

To keep the estrogen at bay

My health was in good hands.

Why twelve traumas now, I don't know,

This was the easiest to explain

And easiest to endure.

How about that?

Cancer was the least of my worries.

Trauma 6—a headache that's lasted 31 years

I saw every doctor in the book

No one can explain

I'm seeing a neurologist now

He is on task

We will see next what has yet to come

I'm pushing sixty and, needless to say,

Everything is falling apart

I could go on endlessly

But why?

Getting old is getting old

I've cured the arches and

The back and hip related pain

My ulcer's gone, hopefully,

My posture has improved

Let's spare ourselves the thoughtless dinner

When I go on and on

About all the things that are wrong with my body.

It will surprise no one to learn

I am conditioned to be a magnet

And I attract them all; they will find me

So be it. Lucky me

# *Self-Love Deficit Disorder*

The gift conception gave to me
Is responsible for every trauma that has taken place in my life
The blessing of self-love was withheld from me
I was unwanted, that much was made clear
When growing up, attention went
to the one who was............................ 'just like me'
My elder born by fourteen months
was an accident but welcomed
She was precious and adored
I stood alone in a cloud of indifference
never knowing why
Affection was withheld, orders became barks
I toddled on through all of this
Understanding that nothing
should be different

This is just who I am

Not knowing the consequences of the neglect that was taking place

Neither I nor them

I moved on through my life believing I Just Was
Who knew at twelve, pen and paper would be my release,
The only way to explore my heart with no one to protest
I never spoke out feelings; if I did, it was dismissed
I was the one who craved attention for neglect of that same need
My thoughts, my words, should be dismissed, as well
While I know that some children behave poorly just to get attention
I hadn't, because I couldn't, which validated my need
To then be even more deprived of attention that

I had never received

Even though I still didn't understand
My feelings were never validated,
How to process them ignored

How to behave despite their being
ignored, ignored, ignored
At this point in time, I made an inward assumption
that 'I Just Am'
Words of others, looks on faces, I studied them well
But none attached to what I felt within my soul
Life was happening inside me, but I didn't dare speak it
Of attention, I will get none
At the age of ten I was molested at the local pool
An older boy I thought I knew squatting in three feet
Was taking girls to his lap and then setting them free
That attention drew me; I craved even that little bit
When he picked me up, he then put his hand someplace
no one else ever had
I'd gotten his attention, I was satisfied with that,
I swam off, went on my way and let the day move on
What I didn't know just then was that a new source of
attention
Had held out its hand
and pulled me into promiscuity

If touching me was what it took, that would be okay

Lie still, don't move, let it happen

In that moment I felt something though I couldn't have said

It's over now and now what, find another

A boy was what I now craved

Holding, hugging, caressing, warmth, affection, kissing

Kiss me please, touch me please was what I must achieve

At home, "I love you" fell on deaf ears, affection was never allowed

To this day that has not changed but my foresight has

Cold and alone for eternity not

I'll find myself the right man

Who will correct my mindset

And treat me with respect

Someone whose mama raised him right

Who is with me for precisely who I am

And wouldn't change a thing

*****

Today, I still am, but with so much more

I've found someone who wants to be with me

You couldn't give me that

Someone who trusts me and needs me

For precisely who I am

No incessant laughing, barking, judging, condescending, or diminishing

No dismissal, no crossed arms, rolled eyes, pivoting and walking away

Just me, finally me, for...

*...precisely who I am*

# from HUSHED DENIAL

# *This Is Happening*

I write these words so fluidly I know not what is next.

What will pop into my mind that I cannot escape.

I need some food, some water, a coffee, and a cigarette,

I'm smoking less most recently, with no effort on my

part.

It belays anxiety. Wouldn't it be wonderful

If that were to become none.

Anxiety, I mean, but cigarettes of course.

Writing out this poetry has become graceful and simple.

I truly do...just write.

I still appeal for an agent for the book that I have written.

Seven months and kinder words each time.

"We must pass; it doesn't fit our plans.

But someone will, no doubt.

Good luck in finding them."

Six queries still outstanding

I've changed the title twice,

I've added new first chapters addressing all the points

In different words each time.

No one's bought it yet.

This is my anxiety, spelling out in words.

Having written a book; these words

My poems are interference.

But in poetry they must be said

Whether I like it or not.

Poetry was what I had when my world fell apart.

At twelve years old, I was raped

but we never spoke of such things at home.

Shame won't let me do it now.

I will not spell out the details; I have done that before

In my own words, in my book

I am done with that for now

My heart and soul had been wounded

But at twelve I didn't know

That the life I'd led had been exchanged

For a new direction. Did it? Who knew?

Fraught with trauma, but again,

with no basis for comparison

I knew my feelings had been silenced

I knew my words would never be heard

Poetry presented itself and I fell in love

All over again

A written voice had just been found

I wrote one poem at a time based on what I'd felt.

The hushed denial was the only possibility.

Hushed denial represents another word, very strong,

Wrong to be spelled out.

The hushed denial shrugged his shoulders,

He so very often did,

I knew of course, it must be him

He must have thrown them away

I'd heard the words "You don't need it."

Spoken before

By a woman who made me wonder

Who she really was.

My heart, my soul, my misery

The rape was in that poetry.

I can't believe it's gone.

Dismissed, diminished, reduced to nothing,

Purely at his whim.

I was still young and I didn't understand

But I knew something was going on.

"You don't need it," he said, time and time again.

Became the sentence he maintained.

Who was he to make that judgement on my behalf.

My clown costume, not long after, disappeared, too

My son's little blanky. My daughter's poetry.

Dispensed along the way

They don't need it, again.

But, I...You don't need it, louder every time.

My children, I suspect because of fear of his reprisal,

Said, it's okay, it's okay.

It wasn't okay. It never was.

It had been wrong for long before

Hushed denial used the words as his mother had before

Many times, in front of me

That must mean

It is a learned response,

It must be.

I did not grasp what had happened

What I was dealing with

Covert abuse as I believe today.

Hushed denial was bearing down on me

And my young family.

When very young, I wouldn't go.

I wouldn't share the custody

With the man that I was old enough to understand

Shouldn't be alone with anyone.

My kids, on weekend visits, without a referee.

Without me?

I fought the fights, defended them

Until I could no more.

I was exhausted, beaten down, diminished in every way.

I told my parents I was leaving him

"Those poor kids. Those poor kids," my mother said to me

"You understand he's hurting them?" I asked

“Those poor kids, those poor kids,” she said

I walked away.

Nonetheless I left, my daughter chose to stay.

This story goes on fully

In that book which now lies upon the floor.

It stresses me to think of this

Anxiety is rapping on my door.

I’ll see this through, I always do, but

I must be done with this today.

# *Hushed Denial*

I know not, now, what I should say

the topic to release in my poetry array

The man of hushed denial came, anyway, at sixteen years old

I couldn't name the world around me, I knew not the word

I knew that something was off with me

I couldn't see it, specifically

I was broken,

My feelings had been dismissed throughout the life I'd led

I didn't know it, couldn't name it

I managed to exist

I just was

I couldn't name emotions but I could feel them deeply down inside

More deeply than I believe

I would have had life been on my side

I'd like to say I fell in love

I know now that I did not,

I was emotionally disconnected.

We met, we dated, we talked on the phone

Dinner, Movies, Family visits, if they were home

I wore his ring, we horsed around

Too young for anything more

I stole his comb, I ran away, he chased me all around

Four years later, nervously, he decided to propose

I said Yes of course, that step seemed to be the next in line

Two weeks before the wedding, a promotion came his way

Two weeks after the wedding, second shift was here to stay

And never left

For twenty years it remained as such

The opposition of our time did not entertain

Four years married we had a son, two days old, first day home

Our relationship should have been done

He became a whole new person

He became his mother's son

Compulsive, controlling, physically unyielding

Was it just a learned response?

Should I take my son and run?

Thirty-two years later, that's what I wished I had done.

I had so many feelings but was conditioned to believe

I was entitled to none

I was no longer working

I wanted to be home with my son

His overbearing discipline always made me cringe

The pulling of hair to make my child face the wall

Then a smack in the back of the head,

'til my baby's head hit the wall.

The verbal dispensations, always to an extreme

"He's stupid, he needs to know it"

"He is four" is what I would say

"No, he's not, he's stupid," which repeated on and on

until

I finally said okay

"You save the dishes for me" he would say

"What do you do all day?"

"What is that bug that's up your ass?"

"Who pissed in your cornflakes?"

"You are sick, you are broke, you need to get some help.

Now stay out of my way."

The mighty, mighty father, had us both under his thumb,

I'd often argue back but that just made me numb

Second child, a little girl, often cried at night

To my surprise, he went to her. She was quiet now

I wish that I had known

A rubber band around her head to hold the pacifier in

Six months old

Should I take the kids and run

This has gone too far

He'd ask me, "Where would you go?

What would you do, you're worthless. You couldn't even get by."

He placed his body before the door

Pushed me down, baby in tow

Four-year-old, sent to his room

Stand off until I said, okay

In his mind it was over with, he went to watch TV

I fetched my son and we all went

Down cellar for the day

I saw the door, I wanted to go, but he doesn't miss a trick,

We could sneak out quietly but where then would we go, on foot?

Older now, my son would ask, why didn't you stop him?

I didn't answer. I knew, my words would just escalate.

I wish I'd told someone when young

To tell the teacher what went on but

fear of the rebellion scared me above and beyond

At seventeen my son moved out

At this point he was safe

Six foot two to the hushed five ten
Enough pounds, the father didn't dare
Instead my daughter came to me and asked me
Why does daddy hit me?
He had taken my daughter on now
So many times, I could have run,
But he'd manipulate the children and
Be alone with them on weekends
At least I could see from here and play the referee
I broke down; I couldn't take it anymore,
I told him time again to go, but he never did
Not my finest moment but I knew
Cheating would end this distress,
Maybe then he'd leave. NOPE.
He would keep the house, the kids,
I should move away.
Restraining order wouldn't work,
I wouldn't want my kids to see
Their father escorted by police
We went to counseling and I laid it on the line.

When I said he hit my kids, he said

Well, yes, but not in the face

I left the doctor's office with

An application for a restraining order

Directions to the nearest shelter,

And the therapist's private phone number.

Daughter 16, brother long gone

I couldn't do it anymore

I didn't want to teach my daughter

    That staying is okay

    with someone with no empathy

    no-way

I kept in touch with her closely.

I knew if anything happened she would tell me.

She always told me everything.

Often, more than I would have wished to hear

But enough to keep tabs on her

Our situation being what it was.

He did and he did and she forgave him

The third time she was done

I took her back home with me

and peace had been restored

A man who had no empathy

And had no remorse

Still believed he held us

beneath his thumb

Until he met another one, a woman who would stay,

A woman who is just like me, she'll deny it to the day,

I, the bitter ex kept my mouth shut.

The new one is beneath his thumb,

Confused, distressed, I'm sure

But still his either way

She, the new one, has no clue, she is my mirror image

It might even piss her off

Get yourself away from it, I say

It's time to run

Your ties to him are different, you would be okay

The house is still in your name, I hope.

Don't show him this message

He will destroy it in your face,

By any means necessary,

When he does, RUN.

# *Blame*

Mom, I used your laptop and something went wrong.

I closed it tight before I knew there was a pen there.

It cracked the screen.

I don't know what to do.

WTF is your F problem

You are F trying to F break evryFthing.

Your F stupid, you must F know that.

You are F stupid you need help

F idiot

It was an accident

You work in IT

Can't you change the screen out

I'll be fine until then

"F screens are F expensive

Do you F understand that

Your F paying F for it

You'll F work it F off"

Words far more barked than said

"WTF is the F matter with F you?"

It was an accident

These things happen

Everyone makes mistakes

It's okay honey.

Go finish your work.

"No they F don't, she F lies

All F kids lie you F know that

She F lying to F now

All kids F lie"

It was an accident.

It was my pen.

Would you please order the screen

F you, no, no I F won't she'll F wait until I'm F ready

When will you be ready

Do you F want my F help?

Yes we do

The you'll F wait

She's so F stupid

Did you get the screen yet?

Stop F asking

I've asked once

STFU you'll F wait

Do you F want my F help

Yes

She'll F wait.

Did you get the screen

WTF IWWY, I'll F get it when I F get it

Did you F punish her?

It was an accident.

She F should be F punished. She F should F be F punished.

She F should be F punished. She F should F be F punished

She F lies. All F kids F lie. You F know she F lies.

She's F stupid, you F know she's F stupid!

She F should be F punished.

She's not stupid, she's 11

Time went on from bark to bark

The screen it finally came

In 20 minutes it was fixed

There is always somebody to blame

For all the things in life

That do not go the way he demands

That someone will never be him.

# *Would You, Could You, Did You*

I have been gifted the blessing of the pen
One, when young, I honed
and I kept every word.
Each piece upon which I'd composed and had often
wept.
All the pieces I had written, mysteriously disappeared.
In the home of only two people,
Just me and him.
Within the reach of somebody
Who deserves the right to say
"You don't need them."
I know that someone with self-imposed omnipotence
Would feel entitled to decide on my behalf and
throw every poem away!
He was blessed with something,
Omnipotence it was not.

I worry when I write these things,

Maybe someone will feel hurt.

But, then, again, why not?

To that I say it just might be my turn

To allow my truth to hurt?

You took all my hard work

Looked me in the eye,

Said "You don't need it" once again.

Unbeknownst to you,

That was just you blowing your cover.

If you can throw my heart and soul away,

Maybe it's my turn to do the same

Why wouldn't I say out loud

You're broken, can't you see?

Do you see that you are a shell of a man?

You verbally have averred

Having AntiSocial tendencies.

I wonder if that's the place to start

Where the chaos begins?

When I asked you, when we fought

"Can't you understand how I feel?"

"No, and I don't care to" after 30 years?

Do you hear the illogic in those words?

When asked if you had empathy

Hushed denial was your response.

Didn't hushed denial suit you best

When remorse was questioned, too?

When with me, I don't believe you did.

I wonder if the rebound wife has any clue

That you may not be

who you presume that you present

What if Dr Jekyll showed the world his Hyde

Only when the doors were closed?

Behind that shield of removal

Away from anyone?

Totally in private, totally wrong?

If, in the public, you know

What it is you should not do

When you get home,

Do you become above

The rules of society?

Do you want her, the new one, to be happy?

Or, as with me, no, and you do not care to

I think if that question were asked,

She would clearly hear your response?

I think that she would understand

that there was nary a sense of

remorse. None for her, none for any

I wonder what she'll do.

Maybe she'll throw you to the curb

The curb to which you two threw me

When I reached enough was enough?

I think, with others you habitually

React with laughter, nothing more

And you become the "great guy"

This whole world believes you are.

Aren't you the great guy who understands,

just laugh,

Don't speak.

Be covert.

At home, the laugh disappeared

Is this when the covert manipulation could start?

A woman and two children,

Did you subvert them all?

I believe I see you as you are

Alone inside your body's shell

Alone is where you are your best,

Accept it and embrace it,

That would be best for everyone...

...now and...

... forevermore.

# ME

# *Broken Beauty*

Once inside a fantasy lie bits of land and sea
A package of great beauty, a gift not born of heed
Shattered painted pottery, fragile, stained with art,
Tossed and disassembled, carelessly torn apart.
Awaiting hands for sorting, a heart with patience to
start.
The tossed up shapes and fragments - into a vision borne
of heart,
A heart attent with discipline, a mind complete in
thought
A soul adept and focused, both passionate and fraught
A work inspired gently from a dance of sanity,
Large picture, tiny wedges, mucilage sans vanity
A portrait of importance to any heart of size
Not random when composed, one bit at a time.
Completed and amazing, wrenching light of sun
Sets behind a waterfall on a night of peace and love.

Bring me to this person who's meant to fix this gift.

Made of mind and reason, gently sorting rift.

Hold me close within that hug, return me to the shore.

Repaint this broken beauty and embrace forever more.

# *The Whisper Of The Trees*

Does a tree live a life, a life like you and I,

One which begins as a seedling and grows so many feet high

Does it laugh and play during its youth, does it dodge the breeze because it can

Or is it a game we will never understand,

That whisper of the trees

Does it celebrate the formation of each new leaf

Does it count every branch and celebrate anon

Does it measure every circle as they form inside the trunk

What is that whisper from the breeze

Is it a language forming or wisdom from beyond

Can the young tree see around it—the tree it will become

Do they share a simple murmur that none of us can hear

Is that the whisper in the trees

The wisdom that man finds soothing when walking down the path
Does the wrath that comes with weather, beating each tree down
Leave damage that forevermore cannot be undone
The storm among the trees
Does it know each lost leaf, each limb that's severed away
Is it lame forever or will the burr evoke its praise
The wind among the trees
Does it mourn each tree as it comes down by nature or by man
Does survivors guilt ring through them all,
shared loss, shared fear of their own impending end
Is it the wisdom of the mature trees, passed down from tree to tree,
which holds them up when one goes down
Is that the silence in the trees
Does it see the barren limbs that hang from a tree that ails

Does a tree stand strong and tall through the coming dying years

Is that the wisdom of the trees

Is all that the comfort I feel as I walk along that path

Does the forest live the life we live and embrace it in its soul

Does the soul of each new seedling hear the wisdom that's passed on

Does the heart of the forest carry wisdom yet unknown

With the woman walking in its shade, while her life moves along

Do seeds and infants thrive upon

The whisper of the trees

# *Save The Last Dance*

Oftentimes I wonder

What this partnership will be.

It's new to me.

I look around and see

Liz's home, this family's home

So, why did he choose me?

My history is colored and when we met, not long ago

I was moving through recovery and I had a way to go

In this past year, everything has taken a new shine.

He has changed the taste of life for me

His business, ranch, and world.

He hears everything I say and remembers what he can

At this age, our memories remember most things wrong

Certain things we can recall

Like the song, "The Dance"

Which played this time last year

And opened up my eyes to the world he's coming from

It nearly broke my heart.

He is strong and happy now.

I'm sure it took some time

To move through his grief

His pain and the loss

 Of the life that he had planned.

The underdeveloped property weighs upon him still.

It was bought for Liz, just before she became ill.

I know by now he'll get it done for his family

 On Liz's behalf.

We hold on to each other for strength when we need

We let each other go to accomplish the work we heed

I wonder if he understands that he is my first dance.

The first man to treat me well.

One without the flaw of entitlement, power, and control.

I had been so beaten down, for so very long

I stepped back and understood that

This is a whole new world for me.

Much family, many friends who come and go as they please.

I like that, I love people, not everybody does,
The men who went before this man kept me all closed off.
Selfish of their own feelings and room for mine, none.
I hear the song, I know the words, I sing along when I'm alone
The end is approaching, faster than we'd like
His wife, his partner and the love of his life,
Is in heaven looking down
Is his intent to be with her, soon
Or is he happy here with me
By his side
Will he welcome death right away
or will he fight to live
I can't know and perhaps it's best
To cling to the words
Life is better left to chance.
Will I miss the pain or will I be the pain
Because I will not miss this dance
It's graceful, light, and fun

First kiss until last breath

Is what is written in the stars

We know not what will come our way

I need him to hear me when I say

Thank you for saving this last dance for me

# *An Angel And Peace*

Words are oft not written when none are meant to say
When one beloved beyond all words has chosen their own way.

This letter unwritten, this song unsung,
Is now being penned, from heart not tongue.

In scrawling and scribbling this message to thee,
A tear trickles down, too tiny to see.

Dear world, I am lonely, my heart overflows.
Past arms open lovingly, yet no one will know.

Sapped of determination, drawn emotionally thin.
No thoughts of good can touch my mind nor thoughts of bad get in.

Time has stretched on and on, I no longer see the end.
Numbness is holding onto me, it is my only friend.

Silence asks a choice be made, the only choice I own.

The only thing within control, my one choice and I know.

I'm sorry for departing, I know you'll ache with pain.

I've found peace beyond this life. I've reached another plane.

I closed my eyes and all thoughts ceased. I'm off to that other place.

Where emotions, thoughts, and long-past dreams will wind me up in peace.

Up there in that clouded sky, amidst the tufts above

Look there for my image and let it speak of love.

Unpretentious silence

A misdirected breeze

Undeterred, I will move on

I'll float,

I'll fly,

I'll breathe.

# Until we meet another day………

I think a phrase, then I pick up the paper and the pen

I start to write but then my hands take it from there

Heart to mind to fingertips, one feeling identified

Named and processed through my poetry

One feeling at a time,

Healing is still in process; a long road yet to hoe

I believe that I should call this booklet

**the Anger I Hide**

Dear Reader,

We are ecstatic to note that you chose to read one of our publications. The time you invested into reading this book is much appreciated. We value your allegiance. As a give back present, we will be happy to share **'YOUR PICTURE HOLDING THIS BOOK'** on our *Official Social Media Handles* such as Facebook, Instagram and Twitter.

All you have to do is – send it to us.

1. Write Your Name
2. Review , if any
3. Subject Line of Email – Pic Holding Book (Book Name)
4. Image Attached – jpeg / gif/ png file.

Email it to – visions.visionary@gmail.com

## Our Authors

Funnel To Freedoms Ring By Andre Brewer
Its Not About You by Jeremiah Valentine
Soft Reflection by Jamie Lim
Where Have All The Bluejays Gone by Jennifer Ayala
Sunlight Reflector by Sarah Cross
Whispers In The Wind by Echo Quinn
Questions We Didn't Ask Out Loud by Mars Hetherson
Walking Through The Four Seasons by Eugene Stelzig
Serving Sweet Tea by Lisa Kendrick
Dispelling The Clouds by Rivka Conway
Summers In Laurel Canyon by Spencer J. Vigil
Burnout by Jeff Kimball
Whispers of Daydreams by April Federico
Unheard Whispers by Dianne C. Braley
The After by Terry Dawson
Joys Of Seasons By Paula M. Rodriguez
Free Air Berlin by Richard Eric Johnson
Homelessness by Crystal Barker
Seasoned Women by Cathy Hollister
Blunder Down Under By Christopher Mardiroussian
The Sounds A Shadow Makes by Dr. Michael A. Roberts
Truth I Must Invent by Francis Diclemente
Shattered by Carolina Herdegen
Desamparo by Crystal E Barker
بی خانمانی: By Crystal Barker
गृहविहीनता by Crystal Barker
The Sounds A Shadow Makes by Dr. Michael A. Roberts
Homelessness by Crystal Barker (Tagalog)
Chrysalis by Alecia Page
Metamorphosis by Susan Baer
Rocky Mountain Reflections By Michael Shoemaker
Finding Myself, One Lesson At A Time